*Behold the rainbow! Then
bless its Maker, for majestic
indeed is its splendor.*
Sirach 43:11

**The intent and
purpose of this volume is to
give you faith, hope and
inspiration. Hopefully it will help bring
peace and tranquility into your life. May
it be a reminder of God's love, guidance
and His many blessings.**

**Our publications help to support our work
for needy children in over 130 countries
around the world. Through our
programs, thousands of children are
fed, clothed, educated, sheltered
and given the opportunity to
live decent lives.**

Salesian Missions wishes to extend special thanks and gratitude to our generous poet friends and to the publishers who have given us permission to reprint material included in this book. Every effort has been made to give proper acknowledgments. Any omissions or errors are deeply regretted, and the publisher, upon notification, will be pleased to make the necessary corrections in subsequent editions.

First Edition Printed in the U.S.A. by Concord Litho Group, Concord, NH 03301.

Treasures to Behold

from the
Salesian Collection

Compiled and Edited
by Jennifer Grimaldi

Illustrated by
Russell Bushée, Paul Scully, Terrie Meider,
Frank Massa, Dorian Lee Remine, Bob Pantelone,
Maureen McCarthy, Dale Begley,
and Robert VanSteinburg

Contents

God's Springtide's in Bloom

There's a lilt in the step
And a gleam in the eye;
There's a song in the heart
And a smile one can't hide.
For the flowers lift their heads
And the birds sing in tune
Since Winter has passed
And God's springtide's in bloom.

There's a balm in the air
And a green on the earth;
There's resurgence of life…
Everywhere there's rebirth.
For the season has come
That will lift hearts with cheer…
It's springtide, glad springtide;
Its message is clear.

Loise Pinkerton Fritz

Let All of the Earth Sing Praises

Never have I seen a rosebud
And not thought of God.
The perfect flower, the fragrant scent,
That grows from hallowed sod.

When I see a magnificent sunset
As daylight slips away,
I'm filled with awe and elation
Watching the crimson, gold-specked rays.

What peace and joy fill my heart
Seeing the seasons come and go.
What glorious gifts come from God
Through the beauty that He bestowed.

Let all of the earth sing praises
To our God who so deeply cares.
He shows His love to us each day
Through the wonders that He shares.

Shirley Hile Powell

Thus I will proclaim You, Lord,
among the nations; I will sing
the praises of Your name.
Psalm 18:50

9

Blessings of Springtime

Blessings of springtime all around,
Everything lovely to see…
Flowers planted, trees in bloom,
Truly a gift from Thee.

Birds in the heavens, singing a tune,
The sun is reflecting God's love…
Blessings of springtime, everything new,
All from the Father above.

Jill Lemming

*Sing to the Lord a
new song; sing to the
Lord, all the earth.
Psalm 96:1*

Pray for Others

Somewhere in the old world
Someone depends on you to pray;
They may not even realize
Your prayers helped them through the day.

And if you ever marvel
At how you always make it through,
You can be sure that somewhere
Someone prays for you.

It's often our prayers for others
That God is tuned to hear,
And just a little prayer for someone
Will draw Him very near.

Gladys Atkins

There's Always Room for Kindness

There's always room for kindness
Inside of you and me,
For opening up our hearts to others
Helps to set us free.

When we do a kindly deed,
Goodness will prevail;
God will never let us down –
His love never fails.

To love is the best example
That anyone can give;
It's worth more than wealth or fame
And makes life such a joy to live.

There's always room for kindness –
A smile, a friendly nod,
But each action shared with generosity
Touches the very heart of God.

Linda C. Grazulis

Only goodness and love will pursue me
all the days of my life; I will dwell in the
house of the Lord for years to come.
Psalm 23:6

Holy Ground

Silently, the bud becomes a rose
In the passing of a day,
And poppy petals softly close
When stars come out to play.
Every garden is a playground
As creatures large and small
Come and go without making a sound,
As seasons come to call.
The reveille of songbirds
Echoes through the trees,
And all throughout the garden,
The melody of bees.

Here solitude and peace abound
Where shrubs and flowers grow,
Even when the leaves turn brown
Or all is white with snow.
God meets us there on holy ground
Where doubts and fears depart,
As we commune without a sound
Together, heart-to-heart.
A garden is a sacred place,
For every seed that's sown
Reminds us of His love and grace,
Through everything that's grown.

Clay Harrison

There Is a Little Miracle

There is a little miracle
In every smiling face,
In eyes that shine with laughter,
Perfected by His grace.

There is a bit of humbled prayer
In every kindly nod,
For showing human kindness
Is a way to honor God.

Nancy Watson Dodrill

Open My Eyes

Open my eyes to the beauty of things
That enclose and around me abound.
Fill up my soul with Your wonders and love,
Of blessings from all that surround.

Alert, may my ears remain open to You
To hear all the sounds of the earth,
Perceiving those things of importance and grace,
Applying their insight and worth.

As I open my mouth, may the words that I speak
Be only of things that are good.
May the thoughts that I think and pass then along
Be only those lessons You would.

So when I reach out to lessen a pain,
To comfort a brother in You,
Through Your healing grace may he know of Your love
With blessings and peace shining through.

Ruthmarie Brooks Silver

*My God, may Your eyes be open
and Your ears attentive to the
prayer of this place.*
2 Chronicles 6:40

17

You Can Be a Sunbeam

You can be a ray of sunshine
Where there is adversity,
For your light can be the spark
That ignites humanity.

Simple words of consolation
Can relinquish fear or sorrow,
And the warmth your love exudes
Will be the joy of each tomorrow.

For caring is a virtue
That somehow illuminates,
And spreads to form an aura
With the glow that it creates.

For those who render tenderness
Are like the sun's reflections,
That warm and spread their radiance
Throughout the world in all directions.

The sharing of your bounty
With those less fortunate than you,
Is the key that channels love and hope
To bring the sun in view.

For God enriched your life with much
Not to keep... but to expand,
By joining other sunbeams
To bring His light unto the land.

You can be that ray of sunshine
To keep God's love lamp burning,
And the power of your one, small light
Will light the world – 'til His returning.

Patience Allison Hartbauer

A Child's Smile

Can there be a greater joy
Of all our joys on earth
Than that a little girl or boy
Should come to us in birth?

Rosy little cheeks aglow,
Laughter mixed with tears,
Tasseled hair in breezes blow,
Mixing trust with fears.

All the joy that God imparts,
Contained in one child's smile,
Lights our lives and lifts our hearts
With blessings for a while.

And as the years slip through our hands,
We strain to keep what's dear.
Oh, friend, make this your heart's command
To love them while they're here.

Elizabeth Rosian

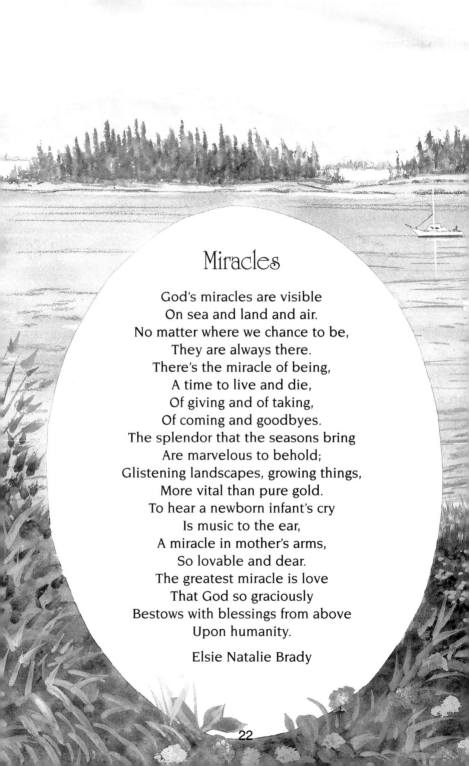

Miracles

God's miracles are visible
On sea and land and air.
No matter where we chance to be,
They are always there.
There's the miracle of being,
A time to live and die,
Of giving and of taking,
Of coming and goodbyes.
The splendor that the seasons bring
Are marvelous to behold;
Glistening landscapes, growing things,
More vital than pure gold.
To hear a newborn infant's cry
Is music to the ear,
A miracle in mother's arms,
So lovable and dear.
The greatest miracle is love
That God so graciously
Bestows with blessings from above
Upon humanity.

Elsie Natalie Brady

They shine through the darkness, a light for the upright; they are gracious, merciful, and just.
Psalm 112:4

23

My strength and my courage is the Lord, and He has been my Savior. He is my God, I praise Him; the God of my Father, I extol Him.

Exodus 15:2

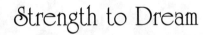

Strength to Dream

Do not be afraid to dream,
For dreams come from the heart –
And when our heart is filled with hope
Anxiety must depart.

We know God's spirit dwells within
A heart that's pure and true;
It gives us strength and guides our feet,
As we our dreams pursue.

We'll find that others, along the way,
Will lend a helping hand –
Will lift us up, ere we should fall,
And support us as we stand.

So let your dreams incite you
To greater things, yet done.
One day you'll reach your zenith
With life's battles overcome.

Mary S. Chevalier

I Know There Is a God

I know there is a God –
I see Him everyday,
In countless little miracles
I find along life's way.

The soft pink mist of early dawn,
A morning bathed with dew,
In every bud and leaf unfurled,
God's face comes shining through.

Not only do I see God's face,
His voice rings sweet and clear
In the gentle tap of raindrops,
A robin's song of cheer.

In the brooklet's happy chatter,
The whisper of a breeze,
God speaks to me each day
In little ways like these.

But more than this, deep down I know
He lives within my day;
I feel His presence ever near –
He's just a prayer away.

God made this lovely world,
He charts the path I trod.
How can I see and hear and feel
And not believe in God?

Kay Hoffman

Autumn Is Her Name

When flaming Autumn spins her magic spell,
I in Fall-flung beauty dwell;
When fields and hills are all aflame,
God said, "Autumn is her name."
When the golden aspens are all aglow
And the sky is the color of blue indigo;
My soul with solemn wonder fills
When Autumn blankets fields and hills.
Oh, Autumn with your winsome ways
And lovely red and gold displays;
I wish your masterpiece could last,
For all your days are unsurpassed.

Nora M. Bozeman

Bless Our Home, Lord

Bless our home, Lord,
And all who enter in.
May they feel heart-felt love
Reaching out to them…
May they find peace and comfort as
They visit here awhile,
And when its time for them to go,
May they leave here with a smile!
May they take the blessings they received
Back to their own home,
And pass on to others
What they themselves were shown…
Warmth and hospitality,
Grace, peace, and love…
That they in turn may receive
More blessings from above!

Millie Torzilli

*Grace and favor You granted me,
and Your providence has
preserved my spirit.*
Job 10:12

A Loving God

There is a loving God
Who makes His presence known
In every evening sunset
And every flower that's grown.

He fills the sky with stars
For that special time we seek.
He sends the rain for our crops
Of corn and cotton and wheat.

Who else could make a rainbow
With colors bright and clear?
Who gives us woods and streams
And all the things we hold so dear?

God never promised us an easy life,
Or even a perfect world.
He only said, "I'll be there
If you let your prayers unfurl."

Our loving God gave us a blueprint –
The builder must be us.
He will make our dreams come true
When you believe, with faith and trust.

Gloria Swan Kennedy

Let Your love come to me,
Lord, salvation in accord
with Your promise.
Psalm 119:41

Some Small Way

If I can bring a ray of sunshine
Into someone's life today;
If I can, in some small way,
Help chase all their blues away;
If I can say a simple prayer
That will encourage an aching heart;
Then I will feel, in some small way,
That I have done my part.

Helen Ruth Ashton

Lord, Let Me

Lord, may I touch
With soft caress
A soul who seeks
Your tenderness.
Lord, let me speak
In gentle tone
To cheer someone
Who stands alone.
Lord, let me work
To plant Your seed…
Bring forth harvest
To meet the need
Of a troubled soul
Who is nearby;
Oh, tune my ears
To hear the cry.
I pray, oh Lord,
I may be used
To lift the fallen,
Love the bruised.
There're souls adrift
On troubled sea:
Here am I,
Oh Lord, send me.

Anna Lee Edwards McAlpin

Give ear, listen humbly,
for the Lord speaks.
Jeremiah 13:15

34

Meditation Time

Morning comes gently in the country,
It is a time of quiet repose.
It is my time to meditate with Almighty God,
He hears my prayers – my heart knows.

A mist hangs low in the meadow,
Diamonds of dew sparkle in the light.
A red, red rooster crows an alarm
To usher the day and bid farewell to night.

A country morning has a magic charm,
Like no other time of day.
It is a time for thought and reflection –
Perhaps God planned it that way.

It seems that Nature takes a big, deep breath
And time stands still for a while.
As I listen to the voices of the morning…
Nature speaks to my soul – and I smile.

Charles Clevenger

Then the Lord looked
upon the earth, and filled
it with His blessings.
Sirach 16:27

36

Count Your Blessings

Count your blessings every day,
You'll find each day there's more;
God's great love extends to you,
Much more than you ask Him for.

Blessings, sometimes, come in disguise
And you fail to know they are there;
But God will lift the hidden veil,
If you turn to Him in prayer.

He blesses you with life each day,
Good food and clothing to wear,
He sends the sunshine and the rain,
For God is always just and fair.

God's door is always standing open,
He never turns away from you,
His grace, and mercy are amazing,
His great love is forever true.

Frances Culp Wolfe

*Grace, mercy, and peace will be
with us from God the Father
and from Jesus Christ the
Father's Son in truth and love.*
2 John 1:3

Count Those Wintertime Blessings

Count those wintertime blessings
For they're all around to see –
The tiny waltzing snowflakes
That entertain both you and me;
The icicles that glisten
Amid the frosty air,
Children tumbling downhill
On sleds without a care.
Snowball battles and skaters
Down by the frozen lake,
Saying goodbye to the last leaf –
Hurray! No more leaves to rake.

A fireplace to snuggle by –
Hats, coats, and mittens too,
Doesn't matter what the age,
There's fun and much ado.
No need to mow that greening lawn,
The ground is marshmallow white;
Grab some boots and stomp about,
Making footprints add such delight!
Peep deep into the forest –
Wee fawns and a mother doe.
What more Winter blessings can I count?
Our generous God makes them flow.

Linda C. Grazulis

Days of Contentment

How peaceful is my little world
When snow outside is deep;
When fields and woodlands round about
Have quietly gone to sleep;
When little snow birds come to call,
Seeking their daily bread,
Along with all their feathered friends –
Yellow, brown, and red.

In the eve, when shadows fall,
It's cozy by the fire.
My favorite chair, the lamp's soft glow
Invite me to retire.
On the stove the kettle sings
As moments tick away.
Contentment dwells beneath the roof;
Let Winter have his sway.

Regina Wiencek

Those Special
Footprints

There're footprints left upon my heart
From people I have met...
The ones who've touched me in a way
That I will not forget.

A gentle word, a kindness shown,
Some laughter we have shared...
Special places we have been;
These footprints take me there.

So when I'm feeling lost and blue
As sometimes I might be...
Then I'll reach softly towards my heart
Where footprints comfort me.

Jill Lemming

Lord, do not withhold Your compassion
from me; may Your enduring
kindness ever preserve me.
Psalm 40:12

You Blessed Us, Oh Lord

You blessed us, Oh Lord, with these beautiful sights;
The Winter solstice and its aura of lights,
The daily sunrises as we look toward the sea,
And the evening sun settings we are gifted to see.

You blessed us, Oh Lord, with the mountains so high;
The farmlands of corn growing up to the sky;
The acres of prairie from here to wherever,
They seem to go on forever and ever.

Wherever I go Your wonder surrounds me,
Whether in valleys or wave crests of the sea...
They prove to us daily of Your endless love,
As You give all of these gifts to us from above.

We are truly in awe as we gaze up at night,
At a starlit sky that sparkles so bright.
The snow gently falling over the earth,
Announcing the Winter season's rebirth.

We thank You, Oh Lord, for Your gift of the seasons,
For each as it changes, Your greatness emblazons;
As I rise in the morning and see gifts of Your wildlife,
I remind myself daily to bless You for my life.

T. C. Moehringer

*Blessed be God, who did not refuse me
the kindness I sought in prayer.*
Psalm 66:20

Go forth into the new day
To see God's beauty all around.
Behold the far horizon
Where joy and peace are found.

M. Elaine Fowser

Daily Prayers

Each morning as I rise to greet
Another day,
I kneel in quiet solitude,
A prayer to say.
I thank God for His care of me
Through the long night.
I thank Him for the miracle
Of morning light.
I thank Him for the sun and clouds
And for the showers;
For all the benisons He sends
My waking hours.

I ask God for the stamina
And for the grace
To meet whatever challenges
I have to face.
I ask Him humbly to use
Me as He will;
To be an instrument for good
Against all ill.
And when at night I once again
Kneel down to pray,
I thank my God for granting me
Another day.

Alice J. Christianson

*I trust in Your faithfulness. Grant
my heart joy in Your help, that I
may sing of the Lord, "How good
our God has been to me!"*
Psalm 13:6

45

But Not My Heart

These feet of mine might some day stray
To other countries far away;
I might search pastures much more green
And find life's beauties in between.
Who knows the path that they might lead,
The times of joy, the times of need,
From fireside joys, I might depart,
My feet might stray – but not my heart.
Who knows the trials tomorrow holds,
The cares and burdens life unfolds;
For days won't always bring a smile
Nor each tomorrow be worthwhile...

Time changes many things I know –
It changes dreams we treasure so,
And yet I've known it from the start,
The world moves on – but not my heart.
There're mem'ries in this precious place
To warm my soul and light my face,
The years have added wondrous love,
'Tis here I prayed to God above.
Whatever else, whate're might be,
This dear old place is part of me,
And though I roam, we'll never part,
My feet might stray – but not my heart.

Garnett Ann Schultz

48

To One Who Serves

I saw the hand of God today
In the brilliance of the dawn;
I saw Him in the flowers, too,
And the emerald of our lawn.

Then I saw Him in another place
So different than before;
I saw Him in the gentle smile
Of one who served the poor.

I saw God touch the vein-lined hand
Of one who could not walk;
I saw Him write upon a slate
For one who could not talk.

Then I saw the hand of God reach out
To touch the broken, too –
Yes, I saw the hand of God today
In people just like you.

Chris Ahlemann

*But the path of the just is like
shining light, that grows in
brilliance till perfect day.*
Proverbs 4:18

For What His Love Denies

God does not give me all I ask,
Nor answer as I pray;
But, O, my cup is brimming o'er
With blessings day by day.
How oft the joy I thought withheld
Delights my longing eyes,
And so I thank Him from my heart
For what His love denies.
Sometimes I miss a treasured link
In friendship's hallowed chain,
And yet His smile is my reward
For every throb of pain.

I look beyond, where purer joys
Delight my longing eyes;
And so I thank Him from my heart
For what His love denies.
How tenderly He leadeth me
When earthly hopes are dim;
And when I falter by the way,
He bids me lean on Him.
He lifts my soul above the clouds
Where friendship never dies;
And so I thank Him from my heart
For what His love denies.

Fanny Crosby

New Beginnings

Each day is a new beginning,
A chance to leave sorrow behind;
A chance to laugh and be happy
For this is the plan God designed.
Each day is a new beginning,
A chance to live life anew;
A chance to walk in the sunshine
'Neath skies of indigo blue.
Each day is a new beginning,
Fresh as a morning in May;
So savor the joy each day brings you
For He has planned it that way.

Nora M. Bozeman

My Little Porch

On my little porch in gladsome dusk,
My spirit calms in the evening hush;
For, though Heaven be eons away,
I know God's beside when I pray!

Yes, He is here, though it's so far
To heavenly palaces, the nearest star;
And hears my prayers, each yearning plea –
For He is close, very close to me!

I feel His presence, near and dear;
His voice in the night sounds soft and clear!
And smell His sweetness perfuming the air –
In my little porch's rocking chair.

So many things I'm thankful for;
My friends, my family, and so much more –
But my little porch adds that special touch,
For which I can never thank Him enough!

Lynn Fenimore Nuzzi

*For the spirit of God has
made me, the breath of the
Almighty keeps me alive.*
Job 33:4

Hope

Never a climb so endless
That you cannot reach the top;
Never news so crushing
That hope will forever stop.

Never a load so heavy
That it cannot be shared by another,
Nor a heart so wounded
That it cannot respond to a brother!

Never a loss so total
That nothing can be retrieved…
Never a hurt so awful
That it cannot be reprieved.

As long as there's a Heaven
And as long as God lives above,
We can find there a haven of comfort,
Of help, and of love.

No matter what the heartache,
However cruel the pain…
God's love will heal the hurting
And make things right again!

Flora Mercil

Happy Are My Days

When I stop to think how precious
The days we have on earth,
Makes me give great thanks to God
Who has given us our birth.

I'll praise His name forever,
No matter what may come,
Knowing that one day I shall dwell
With the Father and the Son.

I'll drink the cup of gladness
And go now upon my way;
I'll follow after Jesus Christ,
For happy are my days!

Dorothy Koeller Wildt

A New Beginning

Now is the time for a new beginning,
Ridding ourselves of all doubts and fears.
Time to move on with faith and forgiving,
Putting aside all grievance and tears.

God is our refuge… His Spirit will lead us;
Stress and anxiety – no longer here.
All pain is gone – burdens have left us;
Sweet peace is ours – God makes it so clear.

We seek new paths… so joyful and daring,
Talents and gifts we surely will find;
And we'll help others with our compassion.
Negative thoughts are all left behind.

Now is the time for a new beginning…
Knowing, through faith, all things we can do.
God is our refuge, our Lord, our redeemer.
Jesus, our Savior, makes everything new!

Edna Massimilla

Into Your hands I commend
my spirit; You will redeem
me, Lord, faithful God.
Psalm 31:6

When Dreams
Are Interrupted

Our dreams can be interrupted
In unexpected ways,
And we wonder what might have been
In these uncertain days.
We're not prepared for tragedies
That turn lives upside down
And fill our hearts with anguish
When peace cannot be found.
We know there's evil in our world,
But there is goodness too;
And God sends down His angels
To light the way for you.

A dream deferred can be reborn
And broken hearts can mend;
For prayers are being answered
And sorrows soon will end.
There are things that overwhelm us
And bring us to our knees;
But thank God we have a Savior
In troubled times like these!
God prepares us to be faithful,
To face uncertain days
When dreams are interrupted
In unexpected ways.

Clay Harrison

Sing praise to the Lord, you faithful;
give thanks to God's holy name.
Psalm 30:5

The Journey

There are blessings beyond measure
Flowing out from God's treasure,
Raining down on us all the day long.
They're sent to remind us
Instead of to blind us;
Sent daily to help make us strong.
We should all be aware
That the blessings we share
With others who travel this sod,
Are meant for us all
As we wait for His call,
And journey life's path back to God.

Margaret Barkley Johnson

A Plan

I stand on the edge of the morning,
Awaiting Your whisper in prayer.
I feel Your real presence within me,
Knowing the depth of Your care.

I peek o'er that edge of the morning
To see what's in store for the day.
Whatever the road I will travel,
You're with me each step of the way.

As I leave this prayer time this morning,
I step out in faith as I go;
'Cause when we are walking together,
Your love and Your guidance will flow.

And when today's journey has ended,
And when I lay down then to sleep;
In dreams to the edge I may tiptoe,
And into tomorrow may peek.

Ruthmarie Brooks Silver

*Whenever I lay down and
slept, the Lord preserved
me to rise again.*
Psalm 3:6

Help Me Stay Focused, Lord!

Please, keep my eyes wide open, Lord,
Except for when I sleep –
To see what lovely gifts You send,
To help those who may weep.
To learn from You, each passing day,
The things I need to know –
Please, keep my eyes wide open, Lord,
So, with You, I'll always grow!

Please, help me to stay focused, Lord,
Through every trial and blunder;
To face my life with all Your love –
Yes, even through life's thunder!
To learn from You each passing day,
To focus on what's best –
Please, help me see the good in all,
And to pray for them with zest!

Please, keep my mind completely calm
To slumber through each night;
To close my eyes, once I confess
Through prayer, wrong from right.
Please, help me to stay focused, Lord,
So I may spread the word
About all the miracles You send our way,
Through all I've seen and heard!

Dianne Cogar

On the Highway

If this life is a highway,
I want to walk it with you;
A journey is much nicer
When the road is shared by two.
If one of us grows weary,
On the other we can lean,
And we'll draw greater comfort
From the good times in between.
I thank God for friends like you –
An expression of His care –
A little taste of Heaven,
On the highway leading there.

Steven Michael Schumacher

The Higher Road

Lord, I want to travel the higher road,
To walk the path that You are on.
I don't need to see the twists and turns;
With You, all fears are gone.

There are peaks and valleys to every road,
Just as there is sunshine following rain.
And if I stumble on a rocky ledge,
Your outstretched hand will lift me again.

Every heartbeat records a peak and valley
One hundred thousand times a day.
Life, too, has its ups and downs
That make us strong on our journey's way.

We can't see the pitfalls
On the road that lies ahead.
But we know the One who's guiding
To the glories at its end.

M. Elaine Fowser

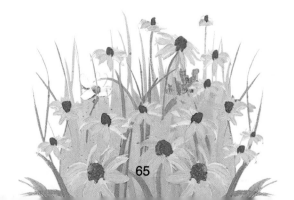

What Is Home

The sound of children's laughter,
A welcome on the door,
A family together
And happiness galore,
With everything so special,
A loving Mom and Dad,
A whispered prayer at bedtime
From one so tiny lad.

A country lane in Summer
That leads around a bend,
A tree that looks to Heaven,
The joys that sharing lend,
It's peace and gentle quiet
Where caring hearts abide,
A wealth of shining moments,
A world of joy and pride.

The little things we treasure
So much we call our own,
The magic of believing
Each miracle we've known,
It's beauty and fulfillment
Belief in God above,
Home is, oh, so many things
But most of all – it's love.

Garnett Ann Schultz

Charm and beauty delight the eye, but better than either, the flowers of the field.
Sirach 40:22

The Beauty of God's Creations

There's nothing like the morning
When Fall, once more, appears –
When scenes of late September
Remind us Winter nears.

The last red rose is fading,
Crape myrtles crowd the scene –
While marigolds are covered
In orange, gold, and green.

The perfume of the four-o'clocks
Permeates the air,
In the early morning hours or
Late evenings – everywhere!

Oh, the beauty of God's creations
Is there for all to see –
When Fall, in early mornings,
Charms me with ecstasy!

Mary S. Chevalier

*A clean heart create for me,
God; renew in me a
steadfast spirit.*
Psalm 51:12

Another Chance

What if today were your last day on earth,
Would it have been lived in vain?
If you could be given another chance,
Would you live it over again?

Perhaps this morning you were feeling cross
And gave someone a piece of your mind.
If you could be given another chance,
Would you be more gracious and kind?

I hope you remembered to laugh today
For a day without laughter is lost.
I hope you didn't grumble away
Without stopping to count the cost.

The things don't seem so important now
That had you so overwrought.
If you could be given another chance
Would you even give them a thought?

Be not too discouraged my friend,
We mortals are all the same.
We often need another chance
To learn how to play the game.

Another chance to help someone
With a smile and word of cheer;
Another chance to be happy
And break the bonds of fear.

Ask the Lord for another chance
Tonight when you kneel to pray;
A chance to prove yourself worthy
Of the gift of another day.

Gladys Atkins

The Lord is my strength and my
shield, in whom my heart trusted and
found help. So my heart rejoices;
with my song I praise my God.
Psalm 28:7

My Heart Is His Home

Adversity may come and knock
Persistent on my door.
I do not worry, for the Lord
Has entered in before.

His presence lives in every room,
Just like the air I breathe.
Adversity can't tarry long;
Where God is, there is peace.

Though disappointments swallow up
My dreams – like clouds the sun,
I know the battle is the Lord's;
The victory is won.

For the Lord has chosen me,
He made my heart His home.
Contented I can live each day
For Him and Him alone.

Regina Wiencek

*I will praise You, Lord, with
all my heart; I will declare all
Your wondrous deeds.*
Psalm 9:2

Friendship Teaches
Us to Treasure…

Friendship teaches us to treasure
Love shared from the heart –
A smile, a deed of kindness,
And, perhaps, a brand new start.
A precious soul to lift us up
In prayer when we're distressed and weak,
And someone to chit-chat with –
Companionship so sweet.

A buddy to hang out with
And oft lends a helping hand
When we feel that we're sinking
In life's unstable, shifting sands.
A chuckle and a joke or two,
A hug to see us through;
All this, and more, because friends care –
Oh, what a true friendship can do!
Friendship teaches us to treasure
The good things in this life,
And faithfully they stand beside us
Through troubled times and strife.
They also teach us to appreciate
A relationship that's true –
Composed of loyalty and honesty
And so much happiness too.

Linda C. Grazulis

Days of Golden Splendor

How fleeting are the days of golden splendor,
When Autumn leaves float gently to the ground,
When Mother Earth again, in calm surrender,
Adorns the hills and valleys all around.

How awe-inspiring are the distant hillsides,
Vibrant glowing in the sun's soft light.
I wish this day would have no ending;
My heart is captured by this glorious sight.

Purple asters dream along the roadside,
Goldenrods have set the fields ablaze.
Soon the quaking aspen will be barren
And blackbirds flock to their old meeting place.

Today the sky is of the clearest sapphire,
Not a lone cloud wanders in the blue.
I've seen many seasons come and vanish,
Yet, each Autumn season thrills my heart anew.

Regina Wiencek

An Autumn Sunset

I count all sunsets beautiful,
Whate'er the time of year;
But none can touch my heart quite like
When autumntime is here.

The sunset's flame of red and gold
That marks the close of day –
A view that is so splendrous,
It takes my breath away.

It's here when all is hushed and still,
Before the vesper hour,
That I behold God's majesty,
His glory and His power.

I humbly bow my head in prayer,
His praises to laud;
O, who can view an Autumn sunset
And not feel touched by God?

Kay Hoffman

Mountains and Molehills

So often it's the little things
That sneak inside and steal
The joys that we have in life –
To see… to touch… to feel.
The problems that we daily face
May never get us down,
And even when the way is hard
We may not wear a frown.
But then again a careless word
May wound our heart so sore,
And we begin to think each day
Seems rougher than before.

And every little fret becomes
A mountain that's so tall,
We wonder how to conquer it,
Or, if we can at all.
So when it's just the little things
That cause us such despair,
We need to know in everything
That God is with us there,
And then we need to do our best
To never ever be
A stumbling block for others' joy,
Or cause them misery.

Gertrude B. McClain

I sought the Lord, who answered me, delivered me from all my fears.
Psalm 34:5

Freedom From Fear

When the storms of life are raging
In the valley of the mind,
And the town is soundly sleeping,
For it now is sleeping time,
Do you think to turn to Heaven,
To uplift your heart in prayer?
Though there's not a mortal with you,
Be assured the Lord is there.

When the storms of life are raging
In the valley of the mind,
And when towns are sleeping soundly,
He's awake… you'll always find.
So when heart and mind are restless,
Lift your heart to God in prayer;
He will give you peace and comfort,
Freeing you from every fear.

Loise Pinkerton Fritz

Now the Lord is the Spirit,
and where the Spirit of the
Lord is, there is freedom.
2 Corinthians 3:17

I call upon You; answer me,
O God. Turn Your ear to me;
hear my prayer.
Psalm 17:6

Communion Prayer

In the silence of this moment,
Lord, please hear our prayer
As we listen for that still, small voice
That lets us know You're there.
May these quiet, precious moments
Connect our hearts to Thine,
So that we might feel Thy presence
As we share the bread and wine.

Grant Thy peace where there is turmoil;
Remove each doubt and fear,
And forgive every transgression
That wrought a bitter tear.
Light the path that we must travel
So that our eyes can see
Every danger and each pitfall
That would keep us from Thee.

In the silence of this moment,
Lord, heal us heart and soul,
And restore the missing pieces
That make the broken whole.
Lord, we gather at Your table
In remembrance of You there.
In the silence of this moment,
Please hear our humble prayer.

Clay Harrison

Guidance From Above

Let us build a bridge for the future
For the glory of the Father above,
Leave no stone unturned
Through the labors of our love.
Foundations built with trust
On whole or part by part,
Bring us closer together –
Open the portals of our hearts.
When we cast away our differences
Scatter them far and wide,
Our bridge, cemented through faith,
Will be safely secured on all sides.
With trust and understanding,
Guidance from above,
Our bridge can be measured
By deeds of compassionate love.

Jacqui Richardson

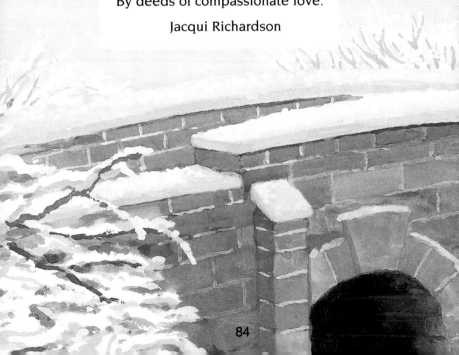

On a Winter Day

When I gaze from out my window
On a world of Winter white,
I turn into a child again
And feel a child's delight.

I visualize on hillsides near
The children with their sleds,
And wish that I were young again
With cheeks of rosy-red.

The snow storm now has ended,
The drifts are heaped up high,
While overhead, a canopy
Of bright blue Winter sky.

I pour myself a cup of tea –
Small comfort for my age,
And in my book of memories
I turn another page.

My spirit is so willing,
But my body won't agree,
I'm much too old to ride a sled,
My style's a cup of tea.

Kay Hoffman

Lead Me Day by Day

Dear Lord, I ask that You will lead
My footsteps day by day;
May I bring warmth and sunshine
To someone along the way.

True loveliness surrounds me
In everything I see,
And when the birds are singing,
It seems they sing for Thee.

The little streams that ripple,
As the water passes by,
The sun, and moon, and stars,
That shine within Your sky.

The trees give shade and beauty,
The flowers with fragrance rare;
These things I take for granted,
Forgetting Your love and care.

Let me feel the Holy Spirit
In my heart from day to day,
And help me sing Your praises,
Every step along life's way.

Frances Culp Wolfe

A Prayer Away

The world is turning every day –
We love, we laugh, we romp and play.
We've grown so busy in every way,
We forget He's just a prayer away.

We ne'er foresee the storms ahead,
From the shelter of our bed.
Each day to us is warm and bright,
But we forget who sends the light.

We search for fame each waking hour,
And forget to stop and smell the flower.
So gather in your heart's bouquet,
God is just a prayer away.

Dorothy C. Deitz

Nature's Poetry

In May the mountain laurels make
A dazzling display
Throughout the hills and countrysides
We pass along the way.
Summer's just around the corner
With blue skies high above,
And all Nature is a garden
Reflecting God's great love.
Flowers grow where no one planted,
Sown by an unseen hand,
Gifts from God throughout the year
That decorate the land.

From the mountains to the prairies,
Wherever people go,
There's something beautiful to see
Because God made it so.
Spring's lilacs and azaleas
Too soon will fade away,
Then poppies and crape myrtles will
Create a grand display.
God created something beautiful
For every eye to see,
That we might know, perhaps believe,
In Nature's poetry.

Clay Harrison

Forgiving

Forgiving will make room for comfort;
Let go of hurt feelings and spite.
Resentments? Let them take a back seat;
The space in your heart will feel right!

The friendship regained will bring gladness;
A sunny day replaces rain.
The wonder and awe of the comfort you've found
In forgiving restores you again.

Ruthmarie Brooks Silver

Remember

Remember all the good things
That happen every day;
The wonderful times of joy
Help bad ones fade away.
Remember fun and laughter,
Smiles so freely given;
Deeds that made a difference,
Made a life worth living.

Remember hours of sunshine,
Not gloomy minutes of rain;
Recall the hale and healthy years,
Not all your aches and pains.
And when you remember,
Please remember to pray,
Thank God for His goodness,
And the blessing of another day.

Ruth Moyer Gilmour

*Remember me, Lord, as You
favor Your people; come to me
with Your saving help.*
Psalm 106:4

Learning to Live

Lord, teach us to fully live
Every hour of the day,
To enjoy the daily blessings
Before they pass away.

May the beauty of each sunrise
Reflect from up above
The renewal of creation
And Thy abiding love.

May the promise of each rainbow
Be a covenant of hope,
When the storms of life assail us
And we must learn to cope.

May the joy of helping others
Ever be our guiding light,
And may peace abide within us
When we retire at night.

May we never cease from learning
Something new every day,
And may the answers to our prayers
Reveal a better way.

Lord, teach us to be patient,
More kind and loving too,
As we truly learn to live
A life that honors You.

Clay Harrison

*Rise up in splendor! Your
light has come, the glory of
the Lord shines upon you.*
Isaiah 60:1

95

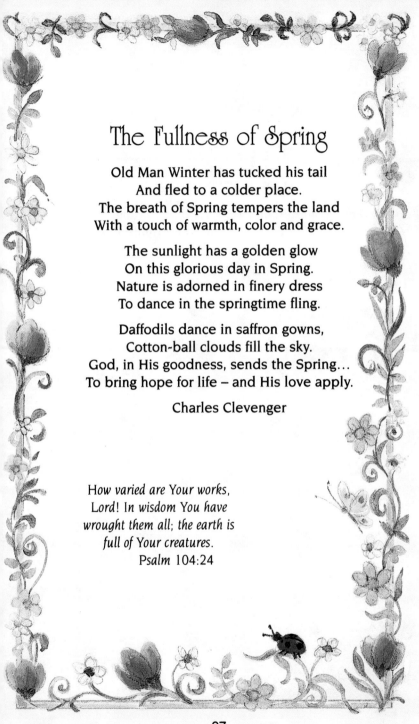

The Fullness of Spring

Old Man Winter has tucked his tail
And fled to a colder place.
The breath of Spring tempers the land
With a touch of warmth, color and grace.

The sunlight has a golden glow
On this glorious day in Spring.
Nature is adorned in finery dress
To dance in the springtime fling.

Daffodils dance in saffron gowns,
Cotton-ball clouds fill the sky.
God, in His goodness, sends the Spring…
To bring hope for life – and His love apply.

Charles Clevenger

*How varied are Your works,
Lord! In wisdom You have
wrought them all; the earth is
full of Your creatures.*
Psalm 104:24

God's Reminders

Splashing colors of each kind and hue
Across a canvas sky of azure blue –
His glory and His power
Displayed at sunset hour,
Each glorious sight, a miracle anew.

The radiance of His artistry on high,
Again, at dawn, looks down from brightening skies,
Breathtaking to our sight,
Earth says farewell to night –
A brand new day is born before our eyes.

After the rain, a rainbow can be viewed –
A holy arc with colors bright and new;
This magic sight is free
For all of us to see,
Reminding of a promise that's still true.

Across the sky, He paints His tapestries
Glorious sights to see in skies above;
Reminders set on high,
Written across the sky,
Assures us of His faithfulness and love.

Helen Gleason

You are my rock and my fortress; for Your name's sake lead and guide me.
Psalm 31:4

Old Things Are Gone

Don't dwell in the past,
Spring forth in the new…
Old things are gone;
Blessings come through.

All things are possible
As God leads the way.
Forget and forgive;
This is a new day!

Greet one another
In God's holy name.
Old things are gone;
New life you'll claim.

Serve as we're needed…
Any place – anywhere…
Love all God's children;
You will stay in His care.

Edna Massimilla

*If you forgive others their
transgressions, your heavenly
Father will forgive you.
Matthew 6:14*

A Servant's Heart

Give me a servant's heart, Lord,
Help me to reach out and share;
Let them know I'm willing
And let them see I care.

There are so many times
I've passed a stranger by,
Not even stopping to wonder,
And not knowing why.

Was I afraid to fail You
And not lend a helping hand,
And be afraid I'd lose
Your footsteps in the sand?

Give me the strength to do
Your will each and every day;
And fill me with Your strength
As I go along my way.

Dona M. Maroney

The Lord is my strength and my shield, in whom my heart trusted and found help. So my heart rejoices; with my song I praise my God.
Psalm 28:7

Beneath the Trees

It's so pleasant in the summertime
To sit beneath the trees
And feel the gentle caress
Of the warm and silent breeze.

And see the soft white clouds
Drifting with the wind,
And hear the crickets chirping;
Their voices shrill and thin.

And to hear the birds so sweetly singing
As they fly from limb to limb,
And feel the graciousness of God
As I commune with Him.

So let the world go spinning by
And do as it may please;
I'll be content to talk with God
And sit beneath His trees.

Wesley Yonts

Good Things Come Slowly

Good things often come slowly –
Yes, and thank God this is so;
If they happen too quickly,
We don't cherish them, you know.
The heart needs time to savor
God's blessings, gradually,
So it can learn to respond
With true thankfulness, you see.
Oh, please don't be discouraged
When God seems to take His time,
Because good things come slowly,
By His holy will divine.

Steven Michael Schumacher

God's Beauty

Have you ever watched a sunrise
That breaks God's day anew,
Or ever smelled the roses
Heavy with morn's fresh dew?

Did you ever see a river
Carrying cottonwood seeds with flow,
Or watch the wheat fields swaying
With the gentle breeze that blows?

Have you ever seen a waterfall
Or snow-capped mountains high?
Did you ever wander through the hills
And watch the eagles fly?

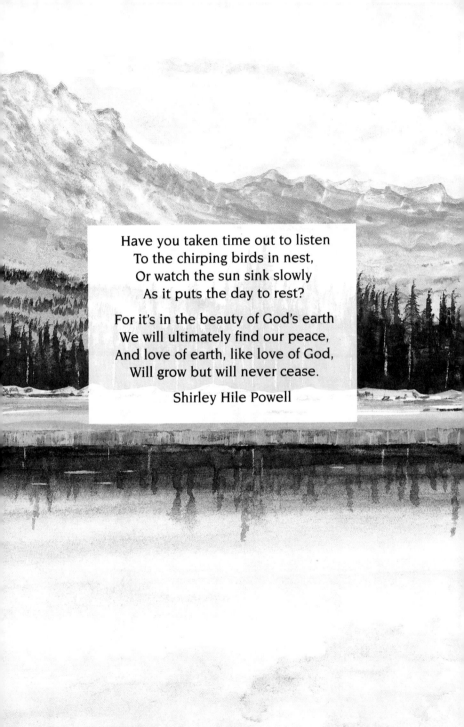

Have you taken time out to listen
To the chirping birds in nest,
Or watch the sun sink slowly
As it puts the day to rest?

For it's in the beauty of God's earth
We will ultimately find our peace,
And love of earth, like love of God,
Will grow but will never cease.

Shirley Hile Powell

Delight in God

Throughout the day take time for God,
Give Him a thought, some praise.
Allow Him to direct your path
All of your numbered days.

Seek out the good that comes your way,
Greet each day with a smile.
Press on anew with confidence,
Mile after obscure mile.

When stress abounds and tries to steal
The joy within your heart,
Sing songs of praise to God on high;
Your joy will not depart.

You are the apple of God's eye
And precious in His sight.
Give Him the cares that weigh you down;
Make Him your true delight.

Regina Wiencek

*To do Your will is my delight; my
God, Your law is in my heart!*
Psalm 40:9

Aren't You Glad?

Isn't it wonderful,
And isn't it grand
To know that you're part
Of God's wondrous plan?

To know that His presence
Ever draws near
To guide and protect us
Each day of the year.

Doesn't it fill
Your heart to the brim
To know that He loves you
In spite of your sin?

Forgiving and patient,
He wipes the slate clean
When we truly repent
And on His grace lean.

In Winter and springtime
Summer and Fall,
Aren't you glad that God's there
To answer your call?

We owe Him our thanks
And everyday praise,
We should love Him and serve Him
All of our days.

Kay Hoffman

I Feel God's Presence

I feel God's presence every day
In so many things I see.
I see His presence in the breeze
As it blows upon each tree.

I hear His presence as the birds
Sing softly when they fly.
I view God's presence as the leaves
Are slowly drifting by.

God's presence can be felt
When the sun shines warm and bright;
And, oh, the beauty that abounds
When the stars come out at night.

I sense His presence everywhere;
Each day is set apart.
God's presence is always with me,
For He lives within my heart.

Frances Culp Wolfe

*You will show me the path to life,
abounding joy in Your presence, the
delights at Your right hand forever.*
Psalm 16:11

Come Unto Me

Come unto Me, the Master says,
All you beset with care,
All you whose burdens seem to be
Too much for you to bear.
Bring Me your cares, and let Me take
Your burdens as My own;
Just put your trust in Me and you'll
Find strength you've never known.

Come unto Me, the Savior calls,
All you for whom life's best
Is but a litany of pain
From which there is no rest.
If you, in faith, but come to Me,
I'll give you courage to
Face pain of body and of soul,
And conquer them anew.

Come unto Me, the Master bids
Those held in grief's dark sway,
Or plagued with guilt and doubt,
Are lost and cannot find their way.
God welcomes all, and promises
The burdened, tired and weak
Who come to Him with contrite hearts,
The respite that they seek.

Alice J. Christianson

Sweet Memories

How I love to reminisce
The happenings long past.
So many beautiful, wonderful things,
But 'things' they do not last.
They pass away in teardrops;
They wash away with time.
Like water color paintings
That once were so sublime,
They fade and all that's left of them
Are blotches here and there,
Like a surrealistic drawing
That Mother Nature has laid bare.
Yet all the sweetness of those days
Can never fade with time,
For love holds them together
Like the roots that hold the vine.

C. Jane Hunt

The Splendor of Autumn

Sunset fills the Autumn sky
At this October time;
Where the mountains meet the sky,
The sundown colors shine.
Evening shadows soon will creep
O'er the countryside,
As the sunset colors fade
Into the shades of night.

Now moonlight fills the Autumn sky
Since the sun has set;
Moonbeams fall on country fields
Where crops are harvested.
God paints all the Autumn land
With splashes orange, red, gold.
He also sends the harvest yield;
What blessings He bestows!

Loise Pinkerton Fritz

*But my God shall supply all your
need according to His riches in
Glory by Christ Jesus.*
Philippians 4:19

117

His Guiding Love

Though steep is the path
I follow today,
The footprints of time
Will show me the way.
For many have traveled
A similar road,
And carried an equal
Or heavier load.
No troubles I face are
New to this earth,
That man has not faced
From time of his birth.

The route has been charted,
And roads have been paved
By legions before me
Who were stalwart and brave.
Their steps never faltered
Nor courage grew dim,
For they trusted the Lord
And let Him lead them.
If my faith and my trust
Remain steadfast and true,
God will guide and protect me
In all that I do.

Dolores Karides

Happy those whom You guide, Lord,
whom You teach by Your instruction.
            Psalm 94:12

Recipe for Life

First, take a pinch of morning sun,
And add a dash of love;
Then measure out a half a cup
Of blessings from above…

Toss in a bunch of special friends,
And add them to the mix;
Then take some hope and precious dreams;
It's really fun to fix…

Roll out a lot of joyful smiles,
And beat the mixture well;
For soon it will be ready, and
Then shortly you can tell…

That after it is baked awhile,
You'll have a perfect pie,
And life will be your favorite dish,
So let's give it a try!

Hope C. Oberhelman

No treasure greater than a
healthy body; no happiness,
than a joyful heart!
Sirach 30:16

Safe in the Father's Keeping

I feel safe in the Father's keeping,
For I know that He does care.
I see Him in all earth's resplendence
That is visible everywhere!

He heals my troubled soul, often,
And great joy to it He brings.
He's pleased if my heart is happy;
He rejoices when it sings.

He gives me friends to cheer me,
To lend a helping hand –
To be there for comfort in sorrow
And always to understand.

God daily provides the necessities
To nourish my body and soul,
And I know He'll continue to care,
Whenever I'm worn and old.

And so, while I am yet able
To lift my hands in praise –
I want to thank You, Father,
For all of my earthly days.

Although life's trials test us
And ofttimes mar our day –
We're safe in our Father's keeping,
If we daily kneel and pray.

Mary S. Chevalier

The Beauty I See

Dear God, I'm so thankful
For the beauty of earth,
For the mountains and valleys
And for all of their worth.

For the springtime and Summer
And the beauty I see;
We owe You so much, Lord,
And I give thanks to Thee.

For the Winter's own wonder
And it's loveliness pure,
With a blanket of white, Lord,
I am humbled and sure.

Everything You have touched, Lord,
Is so pretty to see;
You created with love, Lord,
And I give thanks to Thee.

Katherine Smith Matheney

*One thing I ask of the Lord; this I
seek: To dwell in the Lord's house all
the days of my life, to gaze on the
Lord's beauty, to visit His temple.*
Psalm 27:4

In the Stillness

It is in the stillness of the night
That I try to find some peace;
I strive to hear my Savior's voice
To make my worries cease.

When I place my full trust in Him,
His love is manifested through my soul.
I feel I'm on a higher plane,
As contentment and peace start to flow.

Heaven and earth surely meet
When communion with God is embraced.
I give to Him my heart and soul
In this still and sacred place.

I know with certainty His love within
Shines like a brilliant light.
I have no fear as my Savior
Protects me with majesty and might.

So, in the stillness I find my peace
And lay my head to rest.
I know that in the dawning
I will try to live my best.

Shirley Hile Powell

May God bless us still; that the ends
of the earth may revere our God.
Psalm 67:8

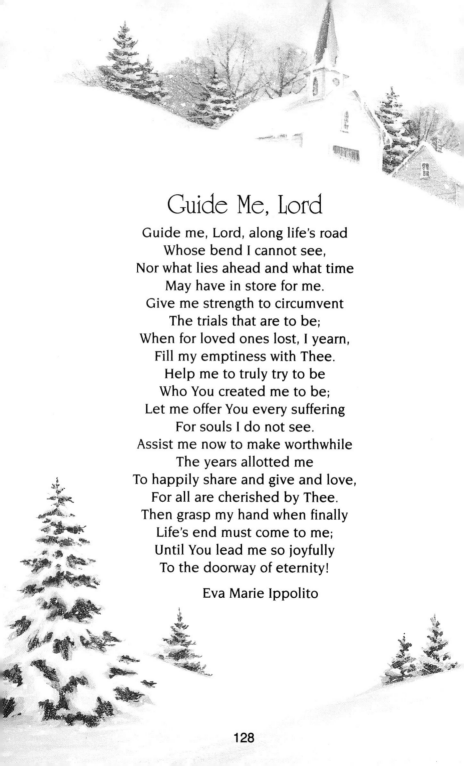

Guide Me, Lord

Guide me, Lord, along life's road
Whose bend I cannot see,
Nor what lies ahead and what time
May have in store for me.
Give me strength to circumvent
The trials that are to be;
When for loved ones lost, I yearn,
Fill my emptiness with Thee.
Help me to truly try to be
Who You created me to be;
Let me offer You every suffering
For souls I do not see.
Assist me now to make worthwhile
The years allotted me
To happily share and give and love,
For all are cherished by Thee.
Then grasp my hand when finally
Life's end must come to me;
Until You lead me so joyfully
To the doorway of eternity!

Eva Marie Ippolito